Our **WILD**™
WORLD
ECOSYSTEMS

ROCKY
MOUNTAINS

Text and Photographs by Wayne Lynch

Assisted by Aubrey Lang

NORTHWORD

Minnetonka, Minnesota

CONTENTS

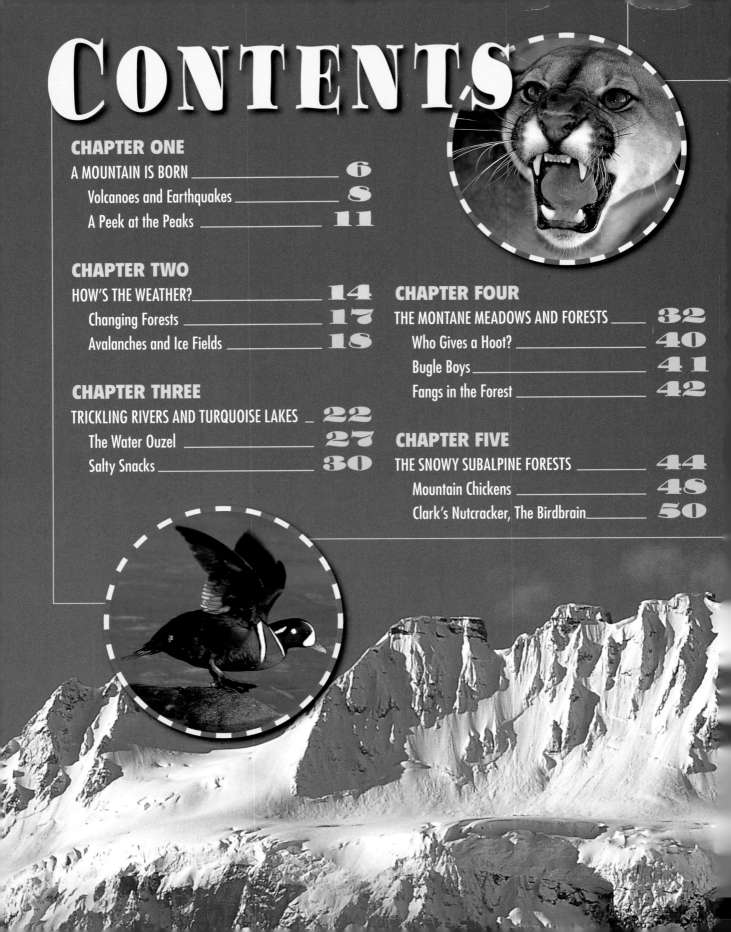

ROCKY MOUNTAINS

For Aubrey,
who encourages me always
—W. L.

© NorthWord Books for Young Readers, 2006
Photography © 2006: Wayne Lynch
p. 6 photo © Cliff Zenor
Map illustration by Mary Jo Scibetta
Designed by Lois A. Rainwater
Edited by Kristen McCurry

Books for Young Readers
11571 K-Tel Drive
Minnetonka, MN 55343
www.tnkidsbooks.com

Library of Congress Cataloging-in-Publication Data

Lynch, Wayne.
Rocky Mountains / text and photographs by Wayne Lynch.
p. cm. -- (Our wild world ecosystems)
ISBN 1-55971-948-6 (hardcover) -- ISBN 1-55971-949-4 (softcover)
1. Mountain ecology--Rocky Mountains--Juvenile literature. I. Title.

QH104.5.R6L96 2006

577.5'30978--dc22   2005038014

Printed in Singapore
10 9 8 7 6 5 4 3 2 1

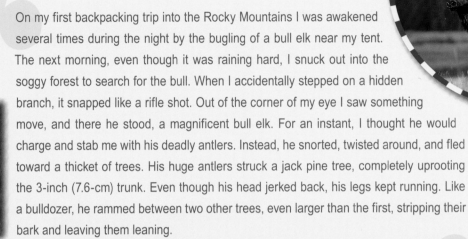

"On my first backpacking trip into the Rocky Mountains I was awakened several times during the night by the bugling of a bull elk near my tent. The next morning, even though it was raining hard, I snuck out into the soggy forest to search for the bull. When I accidentally stepped on a hidden branch, it snapped like a rifle shot. Out of the corner of my eye I saw something move, and there he stood, a magnificent bull elk. For an instant, I thought he would charge and stab me with his deadly antlers. Instead, he snorted, twisted around, and fled toward a thicket of trees. His huge antlers struck a jack pine tree, completely uprooting the 3-inch (7.6-cm) trunk. Even though his head jerked back, his legs kept running. Like a bulldozer, he rammed between two other trees, even larger than the first, stripping their bark and leaving them leaning.

I started to shake. What if this powerful animal had run towards me instead of fleeing? The elk had spared my life. He meant me no harm. He simply wanted to bugle in peace."

A MOUNTAIN IS BORN

I HAVE A RIDDLE FOR YOU. How are people and mountains alike? Mountains are huge, ancient blocks of solid rock. If you stared at the same mountain every day of your life it would never change. You probably think that mountains live forever. So how could a mountain possibly be the same as a person? The answer is that mountains, like people, are born, they get worn down, wrinkled and old, and all of them eventually die and disappear. The only difference is that people usually live for less than 100 years and mountains live for millions.

To understand how mountains are "born" you need to first understand how the surface of Earth works. The outside skin of our planet is covered by a thin layer of rock, called the crust. Think of it like the peel on an orange. However, the crust is not unbroken like an orange peel, but is made of a dozen or more pieces that fit together like a jigsaw puzzle.

These pieces of crust are very large, and some of them carry entire continents. North America, for example, sits on top of a single piece of Earth's crust. Some pieces of crust are covered by ocean, and others are covered partly by ocean and partly by dry land. The exciting part about this whole system is that the different pieces of Earth's crust change position and drift around. In the long

The red fox and the grizzly bear appeared on Earth many millions of years after the Rocky Mountains were born. In fact, both animals walked from Asia to Alaska during the last Ice Age, less than a million years ago. At that time, so much ice covered North America that the sea level dropped and the water between Asia and Alaska drained away, leaving dry land over which the animals could travel.

history of the planet, the continents have changed position often. In fact, the continents are still moving right now, but too slowly for you to notice. Millions of years ago, for example, the United States was located over the equator. Later, it drifted north to the position it is in today.

When pieces of Earth's crust move around, things happen. Big things such as earthquakes, tsunamis (su-NAW-mees), volcanoes, and mountain-building. Earthquakes are what happen when two pieces of crust scrape past each other. If the pieces change direction and smash into each other instead of sliding past, mountains and volcanoes can be formed. When the two pieces of crust are the same thickness, the edges get crumpled and folded into mountains.

TSUNAMI: a large dangerous wave created by an underwater earthquake

Volcanoes occur in a slightly different way. In this case, a thin piece of crust smashes into a thicker piece. The thin crust slides underneath. It gets buried, heated, and slowly melts until the rock becomes liquid. If the hot liquid rock finds a crack in the earth above, it bursts out as a fiery volcano. Later, when the liquid rock cools, it can form a mountain. This is the second way that mountains are born.

These rocks are made of limestone. It is a kind of rock that forms underwater in warm tropical oceans where there are coral reefs and colorful fish. Over time, the North American continent drifted north and the rocks were lifted into the Rocky Mountains we see today.

As soon as any mountain is born the local weather begins to destroy it. Believe it or not, water is the main tool that slowly destroys every mountain. First, rivers carve deep valleys into the rock. Then, rain, snow, and hail slowly strip away tiny pieces of the mountain, bit by bit. When water freezes it swells. If it freezes inside a crack in a rock, the force can split the rock apart and break it into smaller pieces. Water, in all of these different ways, slowly wears a mountain down. Of course, it takes millions of years to flatten a mountain, but no mountain, no matter how big it is, can win the battle against water.

The mountains in both of these photographs are steep with sharp, jagged peaks at the tops. Mountains all over the world look this way when they are young. With time, rainwater and freezing temperatures slowly wear the mountains down. The cliffs on older mountains are not so steep and their peaks are softer and rounded.

A PEEK AT THE PEAKS

The highest mountains in the world are the Himalayas in Asia, and the highest peak in the Himalayas is Mount Everest at 29,029 feet (8,848 m). Scientists believe that the Appalachian Mountains in the eastern United States may have been taller than the Himalayas when they were first formed 450 million years ago. Today, the tallest peak in the Appalachians is less than 6,700 feet (2,042 m). Water has slowly stripped away more than 4 miles (6.4 km) of rock. In 200 million years, the Appalachians will be completely gone. The story is the same for every mountain on Earth. All of them eventually get worn away by water and disappear.

The Rocky Mountains are some of the youngest mountains in North America and the subject of this book. The Rockies began to form more than 100 million years ago when dinosaurs ruled the continent. They were born when the crust under the Pacific Ocean plowed into the crust of western North America. Like a bulldozer plowing ahead, the edges of the crusts folded themselves into tall mountains.

There are many mountains in western North America and not all of them are part of the Rockies. West of the Rockies are the Coastal Mountains, the Cascades, and Sierra Nevadas. None of these mountain chains are as long as the Rockies. The Rockies are the long chain of mountains that runs along the western edge of the prairie grasslands like a wall of jagged peaks. Not all scientists agree where the Rockies begin in the north. Some say they start in the Brooks Mountains in northern Alaska. Most experts, however, think they begin in northern British Columbia, Canada, and stretch 1,900 miles (3,058 km) south to New Mexico, in the southern United States.

The highest peak in the American Rockies is Mount Elbert in Colorado, which stands 14,433 feet (4,400 m) tall. Colorado has 53 peaks over 14,000 feet (4,267 m) high, and hundreds of peaks over 10,000 feet (3,048 m). The highest peak in the Canadian Rockies is Mount Robson, which is 12,050 feet (3,673 m) high.

ROCKY MOUNTAINS

Mt. Robson
12,050 ft.

Mt. Elbert
14,433 ft.

The Rocky Mountains get taller the farther south you travel. In northern British Columbia, where the mountains begin, most peaks are less than 9,500 feet (2,896 m) high. In Colorado, at the southern end of the Rockies, many peaks are thousands of feet (meters) taller than this.

This book is a different kind of nature book than what you may have read before. It's a book about an *ecosystem*, the Rocky Mountain ecosystem. An ecosystem is the word scientists use to describe all of the plants and animals that live together in a community and how these living things are affected by the richness of the soil, the warmth of the days, and the amount of rainfall that wets the land. In an ecosystem, all these things are connected, and all work together. The Rocky Mountain ecosystem is a story about shaded forests, ancient trees, turquoise lakes, and alpine meadows filled with colorful flowers. It's a story about deadly avalanches, icy glaciers, geysers of boiling water, and

GLACIER: a slow-moving river of ice, which may move only a few inches (cm) a year

wildfires. It's also a story about mountain lions and grizzlies, bugling elk, howling wolves, scolding marmots, and hooting owls. Over all of these splendid wild creatures soars the magnificent golden eagle.

As I write this book I can look out my window and see the snowy peaks of the Rocky Mountains in the distance. I have been a wildlife photographer and nature writer for more than 25 years and I love to hike and explore the distant valleys and secret slopes of those mountains. I wrote this book to share with you the beauty of the wildlife that lives in the Rocky Mountains and the fascinating lives they live.

ECO·Fact

The golden eagle is the largest bird of prey in the mountains. Adult female eagles are always bigger than males. A large female may weigh over 12 pounds (5.4 kg) and have a wingspan 6.5 feet (2 m) wide. Such a large, heavy bird needs the strong winds it finds in the mountains to help it glide and soar easily.

PREY: an animal that is killed by another animal for food

GEYSER: a tall, gushing column of hot water that spouts up at regular times to release built-up pressure

If you ever want an interesting way to exercise, I think I know a good one. Follow a mountain lion researcher as he trails behind a pack of drooling bloodhounds chasing a healthy mountain lion up and down the slopes of the Rocky Mountains. I did that one winter in the mountains of Alberta, where I live. The scientists I was working with wanted to study these beautiful cats to see what they hunted and how often they hunted. On a chase like this, expect to run for hours. When the hounds finally forced a mountain lion to climb up a tree so that we could capture it, my tongue was hanging out longer than any of the dogs'. To catch the big cat, one of the scientists shot a dart into the animal's hip as it growled at us from a branch above. The dart was filled with a drug that would put the cat to sleep for a while, and we could then lower it safely to the ground with a rope. It is a rare privilege to see a wild mountain lion on a tree branch, but it is even better to see it close-up on the ground. I loved running my fingers through the animal's thick brown fur which protects it from the winter cold. I lifted its long, thick tail, which it uses for balance when it runs, and I closely examined its teeth and claws. I wanted to know a mountain lion as much as I could.

HOW'S THE WEATHER?

THE FORESTS OF THE ROCKY MOUNTAINS have given me many experiences like the ones I had with mountain lions. It is the different forests, meadows, and rocky slopes in the mountains that give this area its special wildlife richness. Three different factors determine what kind of forest covers a mountain slope: rain and snowfall, north-facing versus south-facing, and low elevation versus high elevation. Let's take a closer look at these factors and see how they work.

Rainfall and snow add water to the soil. Some trees in the Rockies, such as the Douglas fir, need lots of water to grow. Other trees, such as the Ponderosa pine, grow well in dry soil. The soil on different sides of a mountain may have different amounts of water in it. Because of this simple fact, different types of trees often grow on the different sides of a mountain.

In the Rocky Mountains, slopes that face west are always wetter than slopes facing east. The reason for this is that most of the storms in the Rockies come from the Pacific Ocean in the west. As the clouds blow against the western side of the mountains they are forced upward by the steep rocky walls. As the clouds rise, the air inside them gets colder and any water that is in the air falls as rain or snow. By the time the clouds pass over the top of the mountains to the eastern side, most of the water is gone and there is nothing left. That is why the eastern slopes of the mountains are always much drier than the west.

Mountain slopes that face north are also different than those that face south. The southern slopes face toward the hot sun all year round. This dries out the soil and heats up the forest. In contrast, mountain slopes that face north are often in shadow and are cooler and wetter because the sun can't reach them as much to warm them and dry them out.

PREDATOR:
an animal that hunts and kills other animals for food

In a single snowstorm, the high slopes in the Rockies can receive over 2 feet (61 cm) of snow. The soft powder snow that covers these trees is the type of snow that skiers and snowboarders love.

CHANGING FORESTS

Because the northern Rockies in Canada are colder than the southern Rockies in Colorado and New Mexico, different types of trees grow in each part. Some trees grow well in the cold, such as larches, whereas others, such as gambel oaks, grow best where it is warmer. Thus the forests change slightly as you move north or south.

The forests also change when you climb from the base of a mountain to its summit. Let's suppose you are at the bottom of Pikes Peak in Colorado on a warm sunny day and the temperature is 77°F (25°C). At the top of the peak, 7,700 feet (2,347 m) above you, the temperature will be a cool 50°F (10°C). If the wind is blowing, which it often does, it will feel even colder, possibly freezing cold, 32°F (0°C). Climbing to the top of Pikes Peak in Colorado is like going to Alaska. The temperatures in both areas are the same.

Trees in the Rockies don't grow all the way to the tops of the mountains. They stop growing at a certain elevation, called the tree line or timberline. In the Rockies of New Mexico the timberline is at roughly 11,300 feet (3,444 m). As you move north and the temperature gets colder, the timberline gets lower and lower. In Wyoming it is at about 9,500 feet (2,896 m). In Alberta it is at around 6,500 feet (1,981 m), and in northern British Columbia it drops to about 4,900 feet (1,494 m). Above the timberline it's too windy, too dry, and too cold for trees to grow anymore. Only shrubs, wildflowers, and grasses can survive there.

The tough trees growing at the timberline are short, bent, and twisted. They rarely grow taller than an adult man, and most are only as tall as a child. Even so, these dwarf trees may be 200 to 300 years old! One of the oldest trees living at the timberline in the southern Rockies is the bristlecone pine. Can you guess how long they can live? If you guessed 500 to 1,000 years you're not even close. The oldest Rocky Mountain bristlecone measured by scientists so far is 1,700 years old. That means the ancient tree was already more than 1,100 years old when Christopher Columbus came to America.

The alpine tundra above the timberline looks like a grassy meadow. Here, bighorn sheep spend the summer munching juicy grasses, ptarmigan raise their chicks, and golden-mantled ground squirrels watch for hungry golden eagles.

The surface of this glacier looks like a smooth, safe place to walk. In fact, walking on the top of a glacier can be very dangerous because the surface is covered with deep cracks that are hidden under the snow. Careless hikers can fall into one of these cracks and injure themselves, even freeze to death.

AVALANCHES AND ICE FIELDS

When most people think of the Rocky Mountains they think of skiing and snowboarding. In fact, some of the best skiing in the world occurs in the Rockies. For this to be true it needs to snow, snow, and snow again. Many areas of the Rockies receive more than 20 feet (6 m) of snow every winter. That's almost enough snow to bury a two-story house. The record snowfall occurred in the winter of 1978/79 when 70 feet (21 m) of the white fluffy stuff fell on Wolf Creek Pass in Colorado. That's enough snow to bury three houses, one on top of the other!

When 20 feet (6 m) of snow falls on flat ground nothing dangerous usually happens. But when it falls on a mountain slope, it can slide and produce an avalanche. In a large avalanche, 100,000 tons (90,718 metric tons) of snow may roar down the mountain at 130 miles per hour (209 kph). That's like a herd of 12,000 elephants charging down faster than a speeding train. Sometimes an avalanche will sweep an entire slope bare. Trees, boulders, buildings, skiers, and wildlife are carried to the bottom of the valley and buried. In places where avalanches occur on the same slopes every winter the trees never have a chance to regrow.

Avalanches can be dangerous for people traveling on the highways as well as for skiers and wildlife on the slopes. Many roadways in the Rockies have roofs over them in areas where avalanches occur frequently. This protects any vehicles that are on the road when a deadly wall of snow races down the mountain. Specially trained snow rangers frequently check the mountains for dangerous slopes of snow that might turn into an avalanche. When they find one, they use a large cannon to fire shells into the mountain and trigger a harmless snowslide before enough snow can build up to be dangerous.

It makes sense that the northern Rocky Mountains in Canada are colder than the southern Rockies in the United States. Even so, summer temperatures in the Canadian mountains are sometimes in the 80s°F (20s°C), so most of the snow melts completely in July and August. On the highest mountains, however, the snow may last all year round and form glaciers. Mountain glaciers are like hanging walls of ice that lay in the hollows on the top slopes of the peaks. In the southern Rockies of the United States most of the glaciers are quite small because the summer temperatures are too warm to allow them to really grow. It's a different story in the Canadian Rockies where the summers are short and not as warm as in the United States. Here glaciers are common, and some of them form huge fields of ice.

The Columbia Icefield, which is 125 square miles (324 sq km) in size, is the largest field of ice in the Rockies. In some places, the ice is over 1,000 feet (305 m) thick! Seven large glaciers flow out from the edges of the ice field. The glaciers move like cold, thick toothpaste. In summer, meltwater flows through the glaciers and under them, sometimes carving out spectacular caves of ice. Adventurous people from all over the world climb inside the icy blue caves in winter to enjoy their beauty.

MELTWATER: water formed by the melting of ice or snow

Spring meltwater from glaciers and winter snowfalls feeds many of the lakes that trumpeter swans and other mountain waterfowl use. Adult trumpeter swans, pictured here, weigh roughly 23 pounds (10.4 kg) and are the heaviest birds in North America.

ECO-Alert

When humans burn coal, gasoline, and natural gas in their vehicles, homes, and factories, unwanted gases escape into the atmosphere and warm it up. In the last 100 years, so many of these gases have entered the atmosphere that the temperature of Earth is beginning to rise. Scientists call this global warming. If Earth continues to get warmer, many glaciers in the Rocky Mountains will slowly melt and disappear.

Both the hoary marmot and the grizzly bear are commonly found in the alpine zone of the mountains.

Although I enjoy seeing mountain glaciers, it's the wildlife of the Rocky Mountains that gets me most excited. Wildlife in the Rockies is found in four main areas: the rivers and lakes in the valleys; the lower slopes of the mountains, called the montane zone; the middle slopes of the mountains, called the subalpine (SUB-al-pine) zone; and the area above timberline, called the alpine zone. Some mountain animals may live their entire lives in just one area, such as marmots in the alpine zone. Others, such as the grizzly bear, may wander through all four areas. In this

HABITAT: the natural home where an animal lives

book the animals are grouped according to their usual habitats, but many can also be found in other areas of the mountains. Read on to discover the wildlife wonders of the Rockies.

ECO-Fact

Nine national parks protect and preserve the Rocky Mountain ecosystem: Rocky Mountain National Park in Colorado; Yellowstone and Grand Teton National Parks in Wyoming; Glacier National Park in Montana; Waterton, Banff, and Jasper National Parks in Alberta; and Kootenay and Yoho National Parks in British Columbia.

CHAPTER THREE

"Whenever I can, I like to work with scientists who study wild animals and birds. This way, I learn more about the animals and get to have some wonderful adventures. On one such occasion in the mountains, I held a baby black bear inside my winter coat and it fell asleep on my chest. Another time, I helped a scientist put metal bands on the legs of baby owls. I got to hold and pet the family of fluffy birds and stare closely into their yellow eyes. At different times, I was lucky enough to work with hardheaded woodpeckers, slippery slimy salamanders, and grouchy grizzly bears. I never get tired of these experiences. As a boy, I never dreamed that I would someday make my living photographing and writing about the wildlife I love so much."

TRICKLING RIVERS AND TURQUOISE LAKES

MANY GREAT RIVERS in North America begin their journey to the ocean in puddles of melted snow, high in the Rocky Mountains. In Canada, the North and South Saskatchewan Rivers drain 1,000 miles (1,600 km) away into the arctic waters of Hudson Bay where polar bears roam the shoreline. In Montana, the Missouri and Yellowstone Rivers flow east to the mighty Mississippi, and from there to the Gulf of Mexico where their waters

may flood the nest of an alligator in a cypress swamp. High in the San Juan Mountains of the Colorado Rockies, another great river, the Rio Grande, begins as a trickle that will swell and flow 1,200 miles (1,931 km) to the Gulf of Mexico. In another high mountain meadow in Colorado, the clear cool waters flow west and grow to become the Colorado River that cuts its way through the Grand Canyon and finally drains into the hot desert waters of the Gulf of California.

Mountain rivers often look gray and muddy, especially in the northern Rockies in Canada. That's because they are filled with tiny bits of rock the size of dust, called rock flour. The dust is washed into the rivers from the grinding action of glaciers scraping over the rocks beneath them. When the swift rivers drain into quiet mountain lakes, the fine rock flour floats in the water and turns it a greenish blue color. Even on a cloudy day, the lakes glow with this beautiful color.

Tower Falls on the Yellowstone River is 132 feet (40 m) tall. It gets its name from the towering rocks surrounding the falls. The greatest amount of water flows over the falls in early summer when all of the snow melts in the mountains.

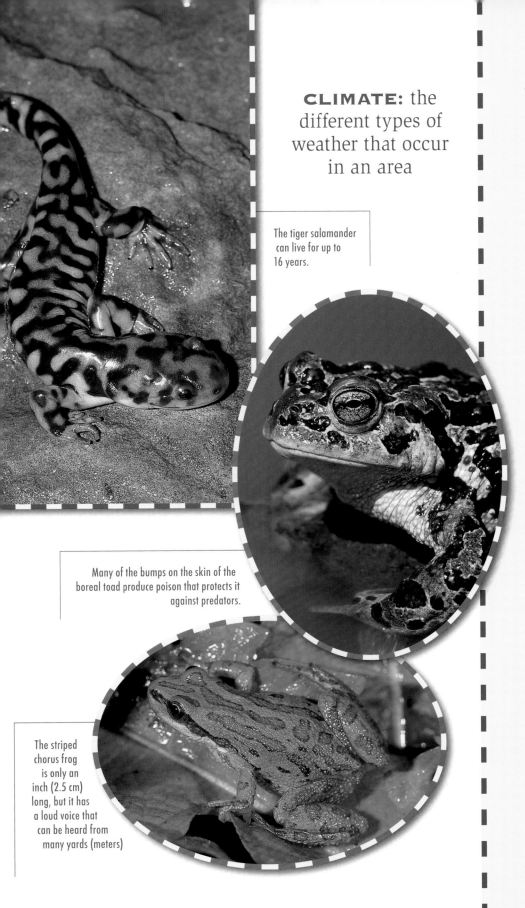

CLIMATE: the different types of weather that occur in an area

The tiger salamander can live for up to 16 years.

Many of the bumps on the skin of the boreal toad produce poison that protects it against predators.

The striped chorus frog is only an inch (2.5 cm) long, but it has a loud voice that can be heard from many yards (meters)

You won't find many reptiles in the cold lakes and rivers of the Rocky Mountains. Most of them prefer to live in a warmer climate. But three species (SPEE-sees), or kinds, of amphibians are tough enough to tackle the mountains: the tiger salamander, the boreal toad, and the striped chorus frog. The salamander got its name because its stripes and spots reminded someone of a tiger. The 6-inch- (15-cm-) long salamander doesn't look like any tiger I've ever seen, but it certainly acts like one in the water. The silent, slippery salamander hunts and gobbles up small fish, beetles, dragonfly larvae, snails, frogs, and worms. When food is scarce it can even turn into a hungry cannibal, and eat other salamanders of its own kind.

The valley bottoms where rivers and lakes are found cover just a small area of the Rocky Mountains, yet this is where many of the birds are found. Nearly 300 different kinds of birds live in the mountains. Noisy blackbirds, marsh wrens, and bitterns live in the cattails along the edges of the water. Colorful warblers and musical thrushes hunt for insects in the willow and alder bushes.

Great blue herons quietly fish in the shallow water, while ospreys and kingfishers hunt from the skies above. Streams and lakes are important to many mountain birds and my favorite of these is the American dipper.

ECO-Fact

The fish-eating osprey (OS-pray) is a crash-and-splash hunter. When it spots a fish, it does something that no other bird of prey does. It plunges feet-first into the water. The bird may dive so deeply that it completely disappears underwater. The osprey's thick, oily feathers keep it dry during such daredevil stunts.

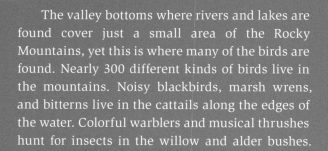

The male yellow warbler is one of the most colorful birds in the mountains. It hunts in bushes and trees for caterpillars, beetle grubs, and other juicy insects.

THE WATER OUZEL

The dipper, also called the water ouzel (OO-zul), is a plain, gray songbird, smaller than a robin. The ouzel doesn't have colorful feathers, and it's not especially beautiful to look at. But I like it because it's a tough little bird, and it can really sing. The dipper gets its name because it bobs up and down constantly as if it were listening to rap music in its head. If you want to see a dipper you need to search for rushing streams and rivers in the mountains. When you hear the water splashing and gurgling past, you're in the right place. Most songbirds flee from the mountains in winter. Not the tough little dipper. It stays in the mountains all year round. I've seen dippers swimming in the freezing water of mountain streams searching for food underwater when the temperature was a frigid -40°F (-40°C).

ECO-Fact

The colorful harlequin duck is different than any other duck in North America. It loves fast-flowing mountain streams and rivers. It's a strong swimmer and dives underwater to feed on insects it finds in the rocks and gravel on the bottom.

The best part about the dipper is its voice, which is really loud for such a small bird. There is usually a good reason for everything in nature, and you might wonder why the dipper needs to sing so loudly. If you think about the noisy streams where this bird lives you suddenly realize why it is such a loudmouth. If it didn't sing so loudly, it would never be heard. You can usually hear a dipper singing even if you are standing 100 yards (91 m) away from a noisy river. On a calm day, you can hear the babbling bird beside a bubbling brook even when it's a mile (1.6 km) away.

The dipper uses its wings to dive underwater and search for insect food among the rocks of river bottoms. It can hold its breath for up to 15 seconds.

One summer, when I was in Waterton National Park, I spotted a bighorn sheep attacking an old rusted car in the parking lot. No one was in the car at the time and the sheep was kicking the rear fender with its sharp front hoof, over and over again. It had kicked the car so often that the fender was scratched and dented. I wondered how the car had made the sheep so angry. Then I saw what the animal was doing. Each time it kicked the fender, dirt and tiny flakes of rusted metal fell on the ground and the sheep licked these up with its tongue. Can you guess why the sheep was beating up the car? It was hungry for salt. The old rusted car had probably traveled many miles over salted winter roads and the inside of its fenders were likely caked with salt.

SALTY SNACKS

All animals, including yourself, need some salt in their diet all year round to keep them healthy. We use a saltshaker, but wild animals must get their salt in other ways. Porcupines will chew on the handles of wooden canoe paddles that have been salted by sweaty hands. They will also attack outside toilets. Our salty urine makes outhouses a tasty target. Many mountain animals, including goats, bighorn sheep, moose, elk, and deer, visit natural salt licks. These are areas where salty water lies in small puddles on the ground. The animals drink the muddy water and also eat the dirt to get the salt they need.

Another place where mountain animals can find salt is in puddles beside the roads. Salt is used on many roads in winter to melt the ice and make the roads less slippery for driving. The salt drains into the ditches beside the roads and this is where the animals go to drink. Every year, many mountain

ECO-Alert

Several different kinds of trout live in mountain lakes and streams. These fast-swimming fish need cold, clean, unpolluted waters where they can lay their eggs and grow. Many people like to fish for trout and they come to the Rocky Mountains especially to do this. Biologists must keep track of the fish being caught. If too many fish are taken, it could harm the ecosystem.

A baby porcupine, called a porcupette, will drink its mother's milk until it is several months old, but it starts to nibble on plants a few weeks after it is born.

animals are killed in collisions with cars when they are searching for salt beside the roads.

A safer place for wildlife to find salt is in some of the plants growing in mountain lakes. Many water plants are very salty and moose often wade into lakes to eat the plants. These large, furry four-leggers will even dive completely underwater to find a meal.

CHAPTER FOUR

It was late May in Canada's Jasper National Park. There were still patches of snow in the shaded corners of the forest, but spring had certainly arrived. Woodpeckers were drumming, bears were leaving their winter dens with newborn cubs, and fuzzy black-and-yellow bumblebees were buzzing about. On this particular morning I was hiking to a nearby lake to look for beavers. As I got near the lake I saw an animal jumping in some tall grass. I thought I was about to be the first person to ever set eyes on a jumping beaver. Well, it wasn't a beaver, but something even more interesting.

The jumping animal was a coyote pup. I had accidentally found a coyote den. The pup hadn't seen me so I hid behind a clump of small trees and sat down to watch. At first, I saw only a single pup, but soon there were three of them. They grabbed each other's tails, dove into the burrow, and then rushed out again running as fast as they could. They pounced on each other and played games of chase and wrestled each other for an old dry bone. My private coyote show came to a sudden end when the mother came home and saw me hiding in the trees. She barked just once and the pups immediately disappeared into the den.

THE MONTANE MEADOWS AND FORESTS

THE LOWER SLOPES OF THE MOUNTAINS are called the montane zone. Here, the forests often mix with open meadows and grasslands, and the trees are spaced farther apart than they are higher up on the mountains. Wildflowers grow well in the sunny open spaces. Many of the flowers have comical

Have you ever wondered why some plants are poisonous? Flowers want to attract bees, butterflies, and certain other insects, which help them produce seeds by spreading pollen from plant to plant. However, plants don't want harmful beetles, bugs, and caterpillars to chomp and chew their leaves full of holes. So the plants produce poisons to discourage these hungry insects from eating them.

names that that make you wonder how people came up with them: elephanthead, silky scorpionweed, creeping beardtongue, and yellow toadflax. It's helpful to know the different mountain flowers because some of them are poisonous, such as red baneberry, locoweed, death camas, larkspur, and orange sneezewood.

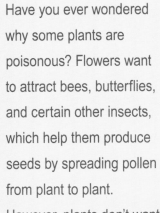

It's easy to see how the elephanthead flower got its name because the pink petals look just like the big ears and trunk of an African elephant. The elephanthead flower has a root like a carrot that you can eat.

The yellow toadflax is also called butter-and-eggs. The plant is a weed that was brought from Europe and now grows throughout North America.

The largest tree in the Rockies lives in the montane zone. It's the ponderosa pine, which can grow 150 feet (46 m) tall and have a trunk 3 feet (1 m) thick. The famous American naturalist John Muir thought the long needles on the ponderosa pine made beautiful music with the wind. This tree has especially thick bark and when the sun warms it, it smells like butterscotch. The thick bark protects the tree against fires, which occur naturally and frequently in the montane zone.

JOHN MUIR: an American naturalist who devoted his life to saving wilderness

The subalpine fir, whose bluish purple cones are pictured here, grows at the upper edge of the montane zone. (Right): The trunk on a tall ponderosa pine may be 4 feet (1.2 m) in diameter. Because of its great size, the tree is commonly cut down for lumber.

The group of aspen trees on the left side of the photograph probably belong to a single aspen plant that has many trunks growing up from its roots. Because the trees are all part of the same plant, their leaves turn yellow at the same time.

Two other trees that commonly grow in the montane are the trembling aspen and the lodgepole pine. These trees have no special protection against fire, but that's okay. Aspens and lodgepole pines grow well in the rich ashes and sunny conditions in a burned forest, and these fast-growing trees move in as soon as the smoke clears.

Many of the highways in the Rocky Mountains pass through the montane zone, and the trees that visitors commonly see there are aspens and lodgepole pines. This might be a clue that a forest fire occurred during the road's construction, and the aspens and lodgepole pines quickly grew in where other trees once stood.

In earlier times, the Plains Indians traveled to the mountains to search for lodgepole pines to support their teepees, or lodges. This is how the tree got its name. The trembling aspen got its name because its leaves quiver in the wind as if the tree were frightened.

The sticky, strong-smelling gum of the lodgepole pine was an important medicine for the Native Americans. They chewed the gum to relieve sore throats and rubbed it on sore muscles, painful joints, insect bites, and pimples.

ECO-Fact

When a fire burns a forest, hungry beetles start to arrive even before the smoke clears. Many species of beetles have special heat-feelers on their legs that help them find fires miles (km) away. The beetles come because they love the taste of burnt, dead wood. Woodpeckers come afterwards because they love the taste of the beetles.

The antennae on the head of a long-horned beetle are longer than the insect's body.

Only the male three-toed woodpecker has yellow feathers on the top of its head.

In some areas, forest fires have been prevented for many years. Logging companies lose money when a fire burns a forest, so they try hard to keep this from happening. Fire, however, is a natural and necessary part of the Rocky Mountain ecosystem. The young trees and bushes that grow out of the ashes provide food and shelter for many different animals and birds. In fact, more wildlife lives in a mountain forest that has been partly burned than in one that has never been burned.

WHO GIVES A HOOT?

At least 10 different kinds of owls live in the Rocky Mountains. They range in size from the sparrow-sized flammulated owl, which hunts crickets and moths, up to the large and powerful great horned owl that hunts squirrels, rabbits, skunks, and any other type of owl that isn't careful. Most mountain owls hunt at night, so visitors rarely see them. One of them, however, is a daytime hunter that perches in the sunshine, in the tops of trees. It doesn't seem to matter to the northern pygmy (PIG-me) owl that it's smaller than a robin. That's because it has the fierce heart of a lion and will attack prey twice as big as itself.

The pygmy owl hunts anything with feathers or fur that it thinks it can kill. That includes mice, voles, and almost every songbird that lives in the Rockies. In winter, the bold pygmy owl often hunts around bird feeders in people's backyards. It doesn't hesitate to grab a little tweety bird that is busy stuffing its beak with free sunflower seeds.

VOLE: a small mouse-sized animal with a short stubby tail

When you are as small as a pygmy owl, even if you are brave and tough, there are many other predators who can make a meal out of you. To protect itself, the pygmy owl lays its eggs inside a hole in a tree, often in an old woodpecker nest. Inside the nest, the owl is safe from attacking ravens, hawks, and larger owls.

ECO-Fact

Surprisingly, the common raven, even with its hoarse, croaking voice, is a songbird. It just so happens that it is the largest songbird in North America, and a common bird of the mountains. Most ravens live 20 years or more. The known record is 69 years!

Male and female northern pygmy owls, like all of the owls in the Rockies, look exactly the same.

BUGLE BOYS

The bull elk, like all members of the deer family, has no upper teeth in the front of its mouth.

No sound in the mountains is quite as wild as a bugling bull elk. When I stand alone on a frosty autumn morning and listen to a pair of bulls roaring across a valley at each other, the magnificent sound reminds me why I love nature so much.

The call of a bull elk starts as a deep bellow, becomes a whistle, then ends with 3 or 4 coughing grunts. Healthy bulls begin to bugle like this in late August and may continue until the end of October. Bugling is part of the animal's mating behavior. It is a war cry to other bulls and a love song to the ladies. I once watched a bull bugle 48 times in just 30 minutes, and that takes lots of energy. When a bull elk bugles over and over again, it is showing other bulls how healthy and strong it is. This avoids fights with smaller, weaker bulls. Bugling also attracts female elk who want the biggest, strongest bull in the forest to be the father of their calves.

ECO-Fact

Mule deer males usually lose their antlers each year in January or early February. The males, called bucks, use their antlers to fight each other during the autumn mating season. Their antlers are not for stabbing. Instead, they use them like hands to lock themselves together so they can push, twist and wrestle with each other to see who is the strongest and healthiest.

Wolves, coyotes, and red foxes live together in many parts of the northern Rocky Mountains. All of them are predators that hunt in the sunlight and shadows of the montane zone. Whenever three closely related animals live in the same location, nature finds a way to keep them from competing with each other too much.

One way these three predators avoid each other is by using different areas of the forest. The sneaky red fox hunts in openings along roadsides and along the edges of fields and meadows. The wily coyote prefers forest where trees are mixed with clearings, such as those created by forest fires and logging. The wolf likes its forest thick and unbroken.

These young coyote pups are just a month old, which is the age when they first begin to explore the area outside the family den.

The howl of a wolf can be heard over a mile (1.6 km) away.

Another difference that separates the three is their diet. The 10-pound (4.5-kg) red fox is mainly a mouser, hunting voles and mice as well as red squirrels and grouse. The rusty-coated fox also eats fruits, berries, beetles, and crickets. The 35-pound (16-kg) coyote is a dedicated rabbit-runner, but it also hunts ground squirrels and pocket gophers. In the words of author Frank Dobie, "the coyote's favorite food is anything it can chew." In some parts of the Rockies, coyotes form packs that hunt deer and young elk. They are especially successful at this when deep winter snow prevents the prey animals from escaping easily. The large, muscular 100-pound (45-kg) wolf hunts the largest animals in the mountains. This includes bison, moose, caribou, deer, and elk.

GROUSE: birds that live on the ground and resemble wild chickens

CARCASS: the dead body of an animal

ECO-Fact

A wolf may howl any time of the day, and in any season. It can howl for several reasons: to locate other members of its pack; to bring the pack together to defend a carcass; and to frighten trespassers away.

In 1994, 14 wolves from the mountains of Alberta were set free in Yellowstone National Park in Wyoming. Wolves had not been seen in that park for over 80 years. Today, 250 wolves run free and wild in Yellowstone, as they were always meant to do.

The winter fur coat of a red fox is much thicker than its summer coat. On the day this photo was taken the temperature was -13°F (-25°C).

CHAPTER FIVE

The red squirrel is a mountain bigmouth. Some of its nicknames are barking squirrel, boomer, and chatterbox. I remember one September when I watched a squirrel all afternoon as it collected mushrooms to store for winter. After it picked a mushroom, the squirrel would climb a small bushy spruce tree and wedge it among the needles. Mushrooms are mostly water and the clever squirrel was drying them out before it stored them away.

They may be clever, but red squirrels also always seem to be in a rush. Even when they are carrying a big mushroom in their mouth they run, run, run. Sometimes this can cause a problem. At different times the squirrel tripped over the mushroom when it tried to run too fast. Once it even bumped its head into a tree trunk because it couldn't see where it was going. At the end of the afternoon the busy squirrel had stored more than 20 mushrooms. I love to quietly watch animals like this. I've learned so much just by sitting and observing. It's fun to try and figure out what an animal is doing and why. Then I go home and read a book about it and learn a whole lot more.

THE SNOWY SUBALPINE FORESTS

THE MIDDLE SLOPES OF THE ROCKIES are called the subalpine zone. Here, spruce and fir trees are most common. The trees grow closer together than in the montane zone, and the forest is cool, shaded, and fragrant. It has the rich, wonderful smell of Christmas trees. Under your feet, the moss is thick and spongy, and mushrooms add color to the shadows. There is little wind in this forest. It is quiet and peaceful, except when you upset a red squirrel and it chatters at you noisily.

In winter, the spruce and fir forest becomes the snow forest where snow piles up the deepest—often 5 feet (1.5 m) deep inside the forest. This heavy blanket makes the forest even quieter in winter than it is in summer.

Snow can also be the destroyer of these forests, but, as with forest fires, this destruction can actually be beneficial to an ecosystem. When avalanches rumble down from the slopes above, it is the subalpine forests that often get flattened. If avalanches occur in the same place every year, the trees never have a chance to grow back again. Instead, the avalanche slopes become covered with grasses, wildflowers, berry bushes, willow and alder shrubs. This is much better food for wildlife than the mosses, mushrooms, and spruce needles that the forest has to offer. As a result, avalanche slopes are very important areas for mountain animals and birds. Grizzly bears visit them in spring to dig for tasty roots. Elk, deer, and moose come in summer to stuff themselves with fresh young grasses, and black bears and birds visit in autumn for the sweet juicy berries. From the destruction of an avalanche, nature produces a wonderful feast.

ECO-Fact

The American black bear is not always black in color. In the Rocky Mountains their fur is sometimes chocolate brown, cinnamon, or even blond.

Willow bushes produce two different kinds of flowers: male flowers and female flowers. These male flowers are called catkins or pussywillows.

47

MOUNTAIN CHICKENS

Believe it or not, all of the mountain grouse wear snowshoes in the winter. Ptarmigan grow thick feathers on their feet to help them walk easier on top of the snow. The other three mountain grouse don't have feathery feet. Instead, they grow reptile-like scales along the sides of their toes, which work the same as feathers and keep the birds from sinking into the snow.

Grouse are big birds that look like chickens. If you start in a valley and hike to the top of a mountain you might find all four species of mountain grouse in a single day. Each one lives in a different part of the forest. The ruffed grouse lives in the aspen forests. The blue grouse lives in the sunny pine forests of the montane zone. The spruce grouse, as its name suggests, likes the shaded spruce forests of the subalpine zone, and the white-tailed ptarmigan (TARM-i-gun) lives at the top of the world in the alpine zone above the timberline.

The male ruffed grouse drums its wings to attract a female.

The eyebrows on the male spruce grouse get swollen and red when it sees a female and gets excited.

Most mountain birds aren't tough enough to spend winter in the Rockies so they migrate to someplace warmer. Not the grouse. They are well built for winter with thick feathers to keep them warm. If it gets really cold, all of them burrow under the snow where they are protected from the wind and also hidden from the hungry eyes of predators.

MIGRATE: when an animal or bird moves to a new area for the winter

In winter, there are no juicy insects, berries, flowers, or fresh green leaves for birds to eat. This is why most of them leave and live somewhere else until spring. The grouse can stay the winter because they eat what other birds cannot. The ruffed grouse nibbles on aspen buds and twigs. The spruce grouse and blue grouse eat the bitter strong-tasting needles of pines and spruces, and the ptarmigan snacks on the twigs and buds of willow bushes.

When a male blue grouse is trying to attract a female it fills its throat and neck with air and booms loudly. (Inset): This white-tailed ptarmigan is slowly replacing its brown summer feathers with white ones for winter.

CLARK'S NUTCRACKER
THE BIRDBRAIN ▲▲▲

"Birdbrain" is an insult that was made up by somebody who didn't think that birds were very smart. However, maybe that person never met a Clark's nutcracker. The nutcracker is a large gray songbird that lives in the snowy subalpine zone. For several months in late summer and fall, it collects seeds from the cones of pine trees and buries the seeds in the ground. First, it digs a small hole with its beak. Next, it puts three or four seeds in each hole, and then carefully covers the hole with dirt, leaves, bark, and pine needles. A nutcracker may bury 100,000 pine seeds like this. Then during the winter when food is scarce, the nutcracker will eat the seeds it has hidden away. It is probably not too difficult for the bird to bury so many seeds. The hard part is remembering where the seeds are hidden, especially when they are buried under 4 inches (10 cm) of snow. The nutcracker is able to do this because it has a very good memory. Try hiding 100 peanuts in the ground in your backyard and see how many of them you can find the next day. Maybe it's not so bad to be a birdbrain after all?

ECO-Alert

Many different mountain birds and animals won't cross a road. They are frightened that a predator will attack them when they are in the open. Roads, power lines, pipelines, and survey lines open up the forest and break it into pieces, like a jigsaw puzzle. Scientists call this a fragmented forest. In a fragmented forest there are too many roads and open spaces, and many animals leave because they no longer feel safe.

The mountain goat loves to climb cliffs. The higher the cliffs, the better it seems to like them. The daredevil goat spends its days leaping from one dangerous ledge to the next. Mountain goats are beautiful animals to watch and photograph, and even though steep cliffs frighten me, I've often hunted them with my camera. I remember one time when the goat got the last laugh.

One autumn I spotted a big male goat, called a billy, sleeping on a pretty ledge and I thought it would make a wonderful photograph. I spent an hour puffing and panting up the mountain until I was almost in position to take the photo I wanted. I decided if I climbed out onto one last ledge the shot would be perfect. As I was getting ready to take the photo I made the mistake of looking down. In my excitement I had climbed onto a narrow ledge that was much higher than I realized. I suddenly froze in fear and hugged the rock. I didn't care about the photograph anymore. I couldn't go back either because I was too scared to turn around. I was trapped.

After many minutes of deep breathing I finally calmed myself a little. Slowly, I dragged my feet back along the ledge, an inch at a time. When I was finally safe I looked back at the goat. He had never moved a hair and was still quietly snoozing away. Maybe he was wondering what all the fuss was about.

LAND ABOVE THE TREES: THE ALPINE

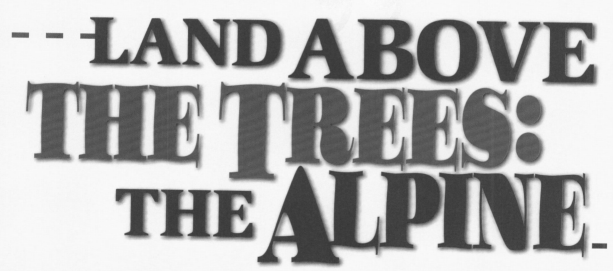

THE ALPINE ZONE IS THE PART of the mountains that occurs above the timberline. In many parts of the Rocky Mountains, the alpine zone is the largest of the four wildlife areas. For example, in Banff and Jasper National Parks the alpine zone covers more than half the parks. Here, the strong winds, frigid cold, and dryness are too severe for trees to grow. It is a challenging place for any plant to live, so the plants that live here have come up with some interesting ways to survive.

Most alpine plants are not very tall. They hug the ground to stay below the full force of the wind. It is also warmer close to the ground. Alpine plants often grow in clusters, like small leafy cushions. In the center of these cushions there is less wind and the temperature is warmer. When a curious scientist stuck a thermometer in the center of a moss campion (CAMP-ee-yon) cushion plant, the temperature was 36°F (2°C) warmer than the air above. Another way for alpine plants to protect themselves against the cold is to wear a fur coat! The leaves and stems of many of these plants are hairy for this reason.

The alpine zone is one of my favorite areas to visit in the mountains. Because there are no trees to hide the peaks, you can watch the clouds race with the wind, and search for mountain goats as they cross impossible cliffs. Moments later, you can watch a golden eagle hunting for marmots, and at the end of the day you can savor the last red rays of sunset as they set the jagged peaks on fire.

The moss campion grows close to the ground in tight little cushions that protect the flower from the fierce winds and cold temperatures of the alpine zone.

Alpine plants commonly have leaves and stems that are red, especially when they are just starting to grow in the spring. The red color is from a special chemical that the plant produces to protect itself against the damaging rays of the sun. It works like sunscreen for the plant. The air is thinner in the alpine zone and the sun can cause more damage there than it does at lower elevations.

The white globeflower is common in wet alpine meadows and along the edges of streams.

NATURE'S HAYMAKER

In many alpine areas, there are slopes covered with nothing but boulders and rocks that have tumbled down from the peaks above. Boulder fields are the special home of the pika (PIKE-ah or PEEK-ah). The pika may look like a guinea pig, but it is a relative of rabbits and hares. Because of this, the pika is sometimes called the rock rabbit. Pikas use the cracks and crevices of boulder fields to hide from eagles, and as a warm place to shelter from the wind and cold. Here they build their nests and store extra food.

Pikas don't hibernate for the winter like sleepy marmots and ground squirrels do. Instead, they stay active under the snow and use the many hidden tunnels and cracks between the boulders.

To prepare for winter, the pika builds hay piles under the rocks. In late summer, the animal is busy, busy, busy. It clips grasses and wildflowers from the meadows next to the boulder fields where it lives, and stacks the plants under the rocks. The hardworking pika may make 10 trips an hour. It usually builds one or two large haystacks for the winter, but sometimes six. Each one can contain a bushel basket full of dried plants. When winter snows finally cover the ground the pika has lots of extra food while it waits for spring to return.

ECO-Fact

The hoary marmot is the largest squirrel in North America. It lives in rocky slopes, often in the alpine zone. This 15-pound (7-kg) squirrel lives in the northern Rocky Mountains. Its smaller cousin, the yellow-bellied marmot, lives in the southern Rockies. Up in the cold, snowy alpine zone of the northern Rockies, the hoary marmot may hibernate for eight months every winter.

The pika is very sensitive to heat. During the warm summer, it is active mainly in the cooler hours of early morning and late afternoon.

CLIMBING BLACK BEARS AND
DIGGING GRIZZLIES

Black bears rarely roam far from trees, especially in the same mountains where grizzlies live. That's because black bears are frightened of grizzlies and they feel safest when there are trees nearby that they can climb to escape from an attacking grizzly. Grizzly bears roam everywhere in the mountains, but they especially like the alpine zone. Here they can dig up the roots of some of their favorite foods such as glacier lilies, wild onions, spring beauties, peavines, and Indian rice.

Black bears are built to climb, whereas grizzly bears are built to dig. The hump above a grizzly's shoulders is made of thick muscles, which the animal uses when it digs. The claws on a grizzly's front feet are much longer than those on a black bear. Sometimes, they can be as long as a ballpoint pen!

PEAVINE: a mountain plant with a juicy root that animals like to eat

Once, I watched a mother grizzly tear up an alpine meadow as she dug for peavine roots. The bear would dig her front claws into the soil, then rock backward with her entire weight. After she had lifted up a section of earth she would flip it upside down. Then she would carefully scrape away the dirt with her claws, and nibble off the tasty roots that she found. The mother grizzly bear had two young cubs with her. The bear cubs mostly ran around and played, since they were still young enough to be drinking their mother's milk and probably not too hungry. Even so, they often sniffed the dirt where their mother had been digging and they would sometimes chew on a root. In this way the cubs were learning which foods were good to eat.

The grizzly above is digging for roots, and this two-month-old black bear cub is just learning to climb.

If you have ever accidentally bumped your head you know how much it can hurt. So how do rams ram their heads together without hurting themselves? The bighorn has a thick skull filled with air pockets that absorb the shock of these collisions and usually keep the animals from injuring themselves. Young rams just learning to fight, however, may sometimes crack their skulls and even die during these battles.

ALPINE ▲ ▲
BONEHEADS

Alpine meadows are a popular place for male bighorn sheep, called rams, to gather for the autumn mating season. The rams fight each other by banging heads to see who is the biggest and strongest bonehead in the bunch. The winner gets to mate with any female sheep nearby. The sound of rams smashing their heads together as hard as they can sounds like a gunshot and can be heard a mile (1.6 km) away. The hardheaded sheep may ram into each other a dozen times until one of them finally quits and runs away.

Wildlife lives in a different world than we do. It is a world we are only beginning to understand. I have spent my life watching wildlife in the mountains and around the world, and I am constantly surprised and amazed. In the mountains in spring I watched a handsome blue grouse hoot and strut when I was just a few feet (meters) away. I remember the beauty of a great gray owl as it hunted in a snowstorm, and the curious stare of a pine marten as it hid among the golden needles of a larch tree in autumn. I will never forget following a bull moose for an entire day as it courted a female or watching an osprey dive for a fish and disappear in a splash of silver water. These are just a few of the mountain memories I treasure. I hope there will always be wild mountains for you to discover and enjoy.

ROCKY MOUNTAIN WEB SITES

If you want to learn more about the Rocky Mountains and the wildlife that lives there, you can search the Internet for the web sites I have listed below. This is where you can learn about the problems facing the mountains, what people are doing to save them, and how you can help.

Banff National Park, Alberta
www.pc.gc.ca/pn-np/ab/banff/index_e.asp

Glacier National Park, Montana
www.nps.gov/glac/

Grand Teton National Park, Wyoming
www.nps.gov/grte/

Jasper National Park, Alberta
www.pc.gc.ca/pn-np/ab/jasper/index_e.asp

Kootenay National Park, British Columbia
www.pc.gc.ca/pn-np/bc/kootenay/index_e.asp

National Elk Refuge
www.fws.gov/nationalelkrefuge/

National Parks and Conservation Association
www.npca.org/

Rocky Mountain Elk Foundation
www.rmef.org/

Rocky Mountain National Park, Colorado
www.nps.gov/romo/

Waterton Lakes National Park, Alberta
www.pc.gc.ca/pn-np/ab/waterton/index_e.asp

Yellowstone National Park, Wyoming
www.nps.gov/yell/

Yoho National Park, British Columbia
www.pc.gc.ca/pn-np/bc/Yoho/index_e.asp

When DR. WAYNE LYNCH met AUBREY LANG, he was an emergency doctor and she was a pediatric nurse. Within five years they were married and had left their jobs in medicine to work together as writers and wildlife photographers. For twenty-seven years they have explored the great wilderness areas of the world—tropical rainforests, remote islands in the Arctic and Antarctic, deserts, mountains, prairies, and African plains.

Dr. Lynch is a popular guest lecturer and an award-winning science writer. His books cover a wide range of subjects, including the biology and behavior of owls, penguins, and northern bears; arctic, boreal, and grassland ecology; and the lives of prairie birds and mountain wildlife. He is a fellow of the internationally recognized Explorers Club, and an elected Fellow of the prestigious Arctic Institute of North America.

Dr. Lynch has written the texts and taken the photographs for five other titles in NorthWord's Our Wild World animal series: *Seals, Hawks, Owls, Vultures,* and *Falcons*.